More Christmas Piano Solos

For All Piano Methods

Table of Contents

Book: ISBN 978-1-4234-8362-5
Book/CD: ISBN 978-1-4234-9327-3

HAL•LEONARD®
CORPORATION
7777 W. BLUEMOUND RD. P.O. BOX 13819 MILWAUKEE, WI 53213

Visit Hal Leonard Online at
www.halleonard.com

We Are Santa's Elves

Music and Lyrics by
Johnny Marks
Arranged by Phillip Keveren

Accompaniment (Student plays one octave higher than written.) TRACKS 1/2

we are San-ta's elves! We work hard all day,

but our work is play. Dolls we try out, see if they cry out,

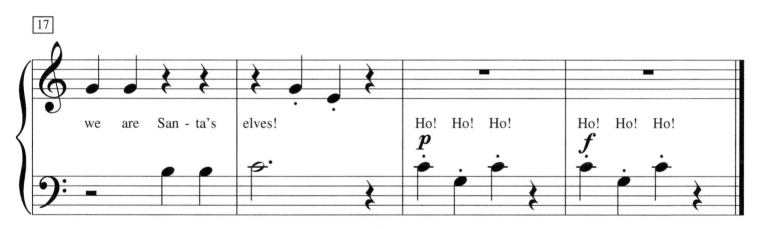

we are San-ta's elves! Ho! Ho! Ho! Ho! Ho! Ho!

p f

pp mf

3

Silver Bells

from the Paramount Picture THE LEMON DROP KID

Words and Music by Jay Livingston
and Ray Evans
Arranged by Phillip Keveren

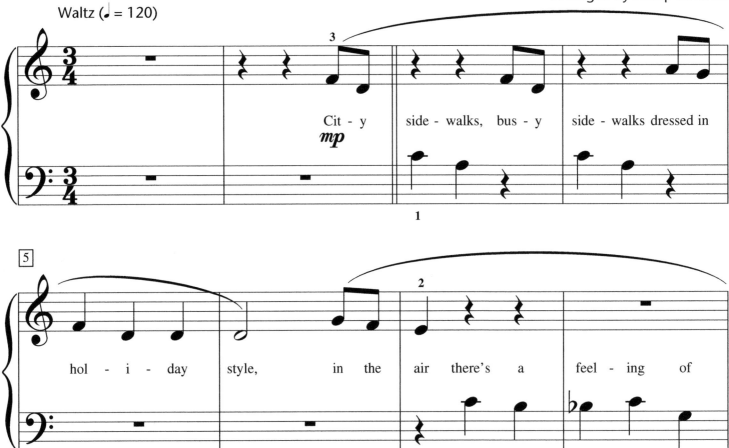

Cit - y side - walks, bus - y side - walks dressed in hol - i - day style, in the air there's a feel - ing of

Accompaniment (Student plays one octave higher than written.) TRACKS 3/4

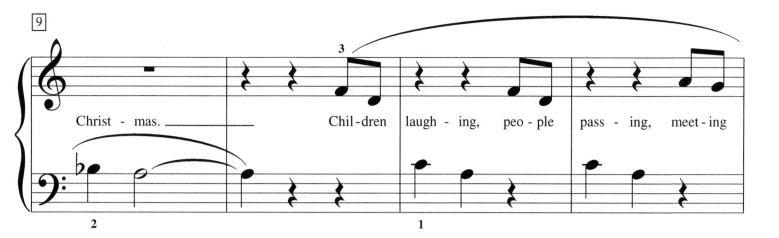

Christ - mas. _____ Chil -dren laugh - ing, peo - ple pass - ing, meet -ing

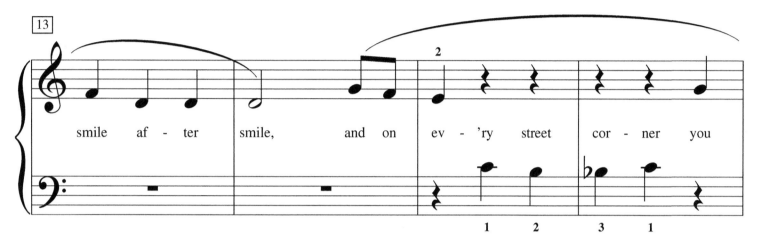

smile af - ter smile, and on ev - 'ry street cor - ner you

hear: _____ Sil - ver bells, _____

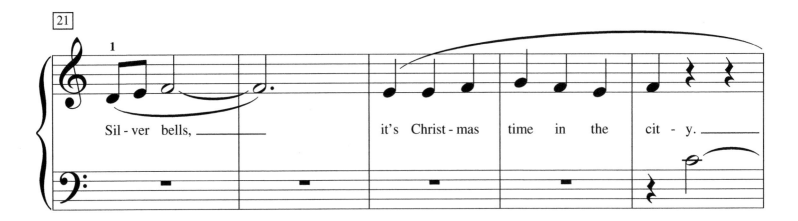

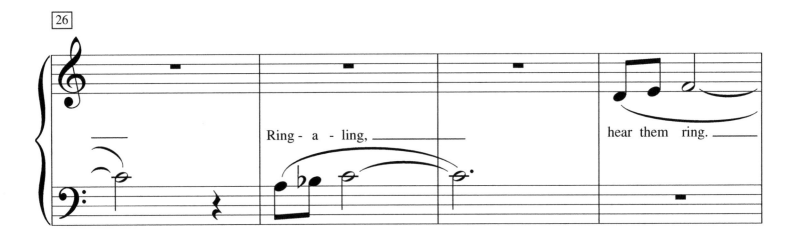

Sil - ver bells, _____ it's Christ - mas time in the cit - y. _____

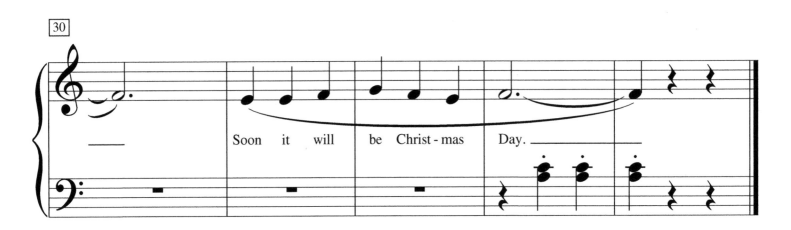

Ring - a - ling, _____ hear them ring. _____

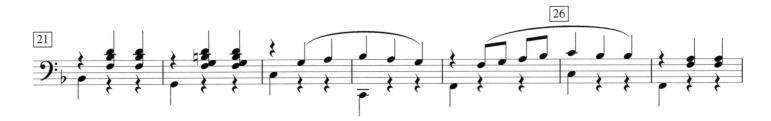

Soon it will be Christ - mas Day. _____

A Holly Jolly Christmas

Music and Lyrics by
Johnny Marks
Arranged by Fred Kern

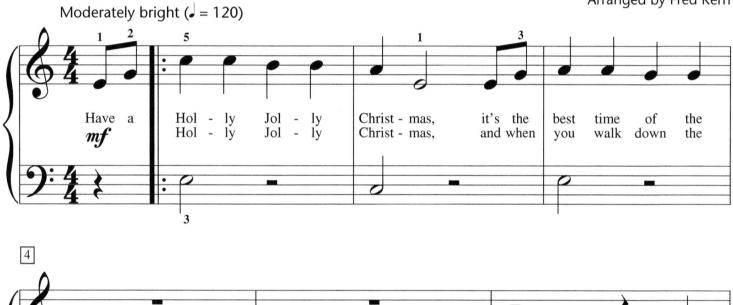

Moderately bright (♩ = 120)

Have a | Hol – ly Jol – ly | Christ – mas, it's the | best time of the
Hol – ly Jol – ly | Christ – mas, and when | you walk down the

year. | I don't know if | there'll be snow, but
street | say hel – lo to | friends you know and

Accompaniment (Student plays one octave higher than written.) 🔘 **TRACKS 5/6**

Moderately bright (♩ = 120)

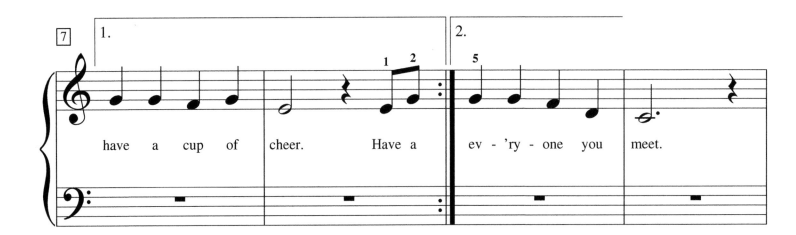

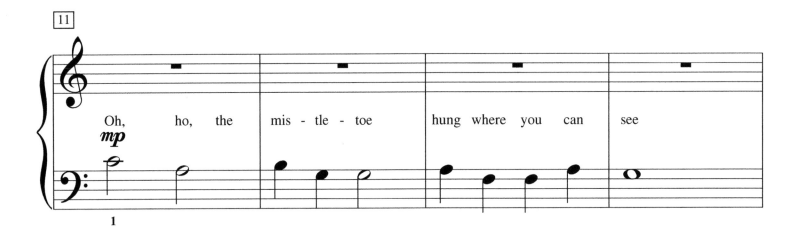

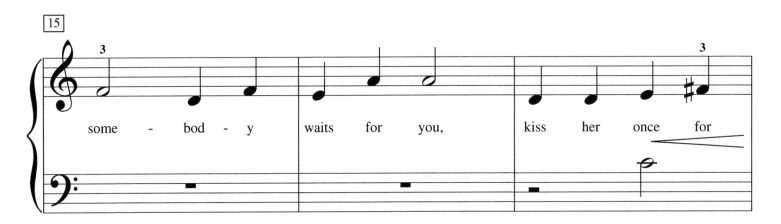

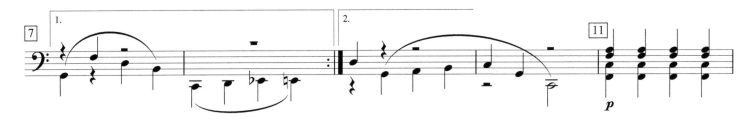

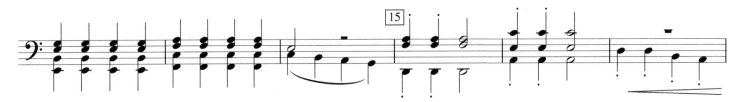

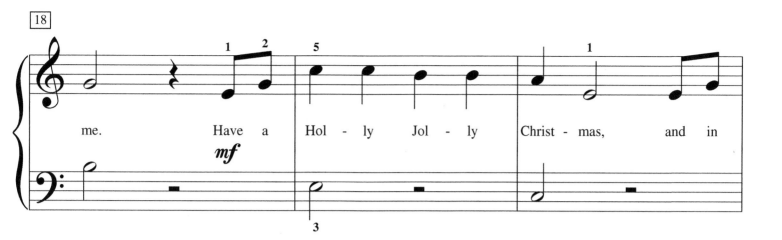

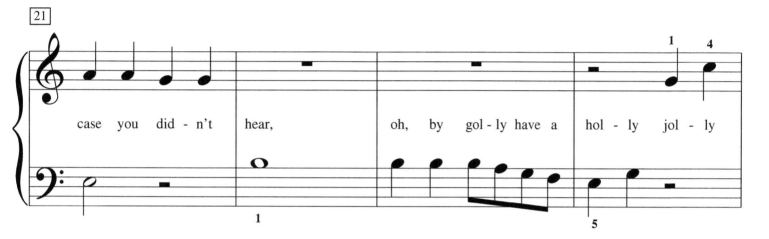

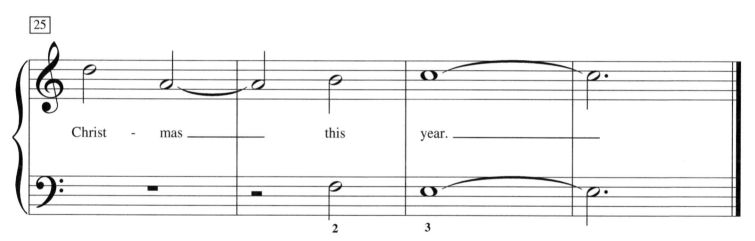

I Want a Hippopotamus for Christmas

(Hippo the Hero)

Words and Music by
John Rox
Arranged by Jennifer Linn

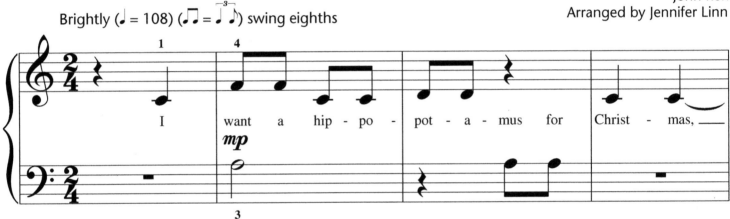

Accompaniment (Student plays one octave higher than written.)

TRACKS
7/8

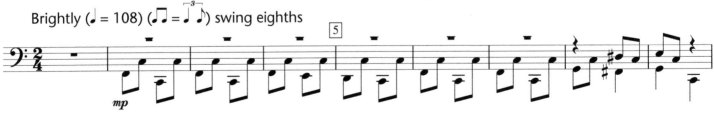

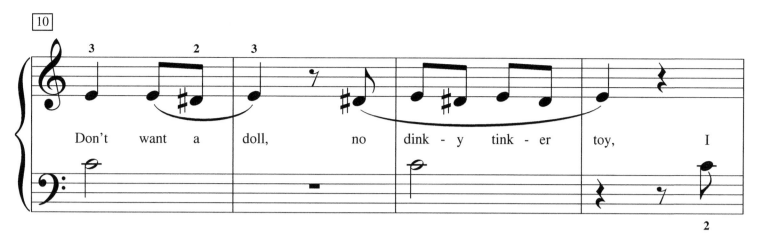

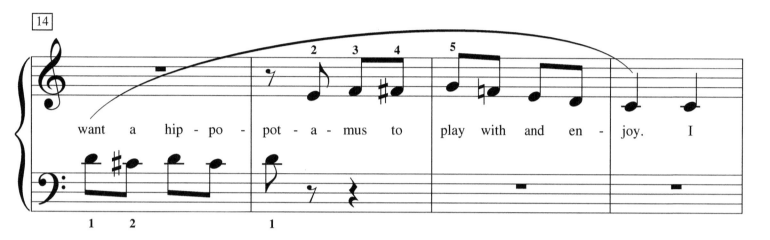

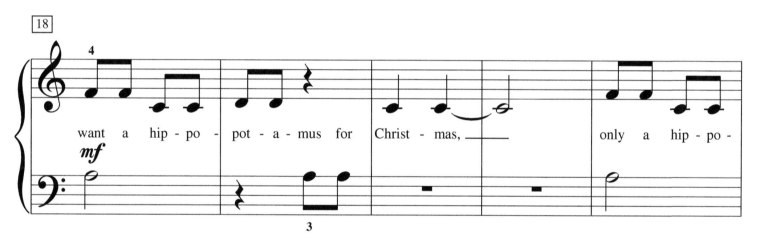

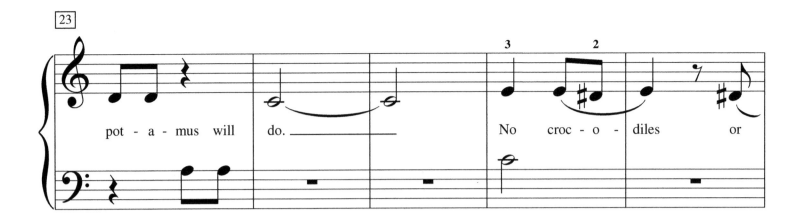

pot - a - mus will do. _____ No croc - o - diles or

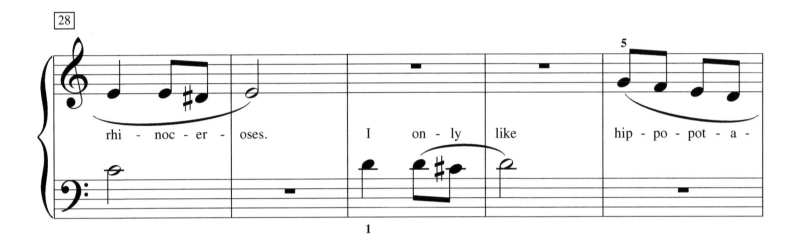

rhi - noc - er - oses. I on - ly like hip - po - pot - a -

muses and hip - po - pot - a - mus - es like me too. _____

Angels We Have Heard on High

Traditional French Carol
Translated by James Chadwick
Arranged by Carol Klose

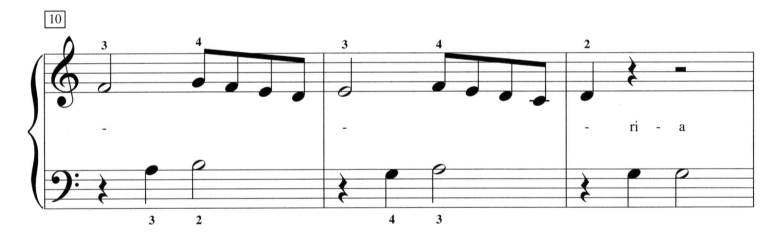

ech - o - ing their | joy - ous strains.⎫
which in - spire your | heav'n - ly song?⎭ | Glo -

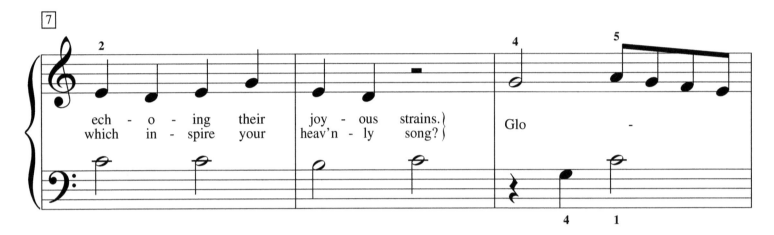

- | - | - ri - a

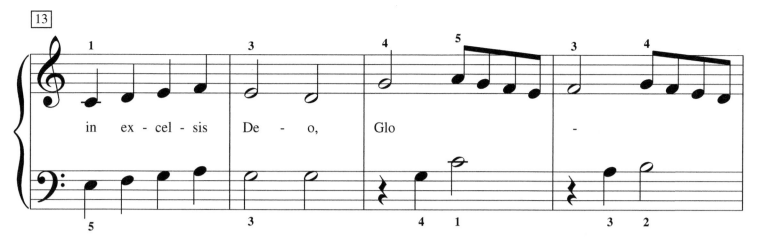

in ex - cel - sis De - o, Glo -

- ri - a in ex - cel - sis

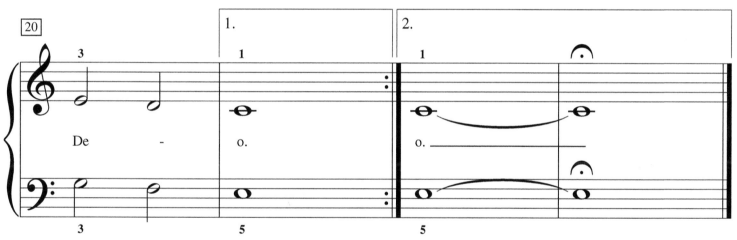

De - o.

Let It Snow! Let It Snow! Let It Snow!

Words by Sammy Cahn
Music by Jule Styne
Arranged by Carol Klose

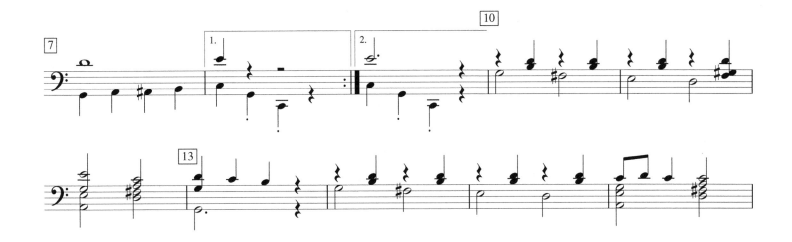

warm. The fire is slow - ly dy - ing, and my

dear, we're still good - bye - ing, but as long as you love me

so, let it snow, let it snow, let it snow.

Auld Lang Syne

Words by Robert Burns
Traditional Scottish Melody
Arranged by Fred Kern

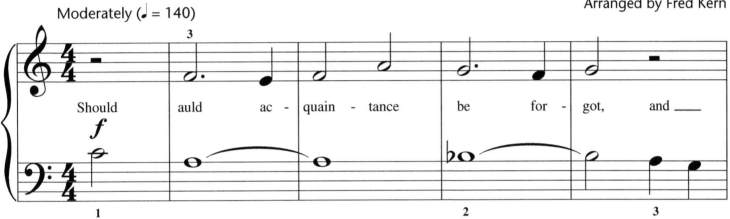

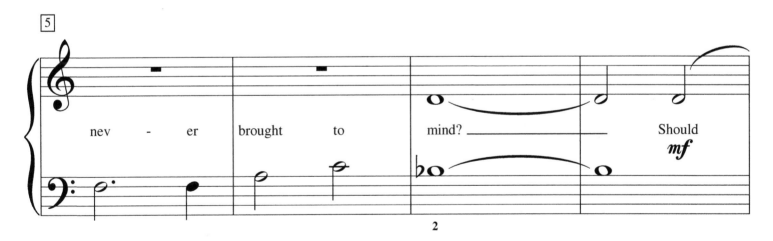

Accompaniment (Student plays one octave higher than written.)

TRACKS
13/14

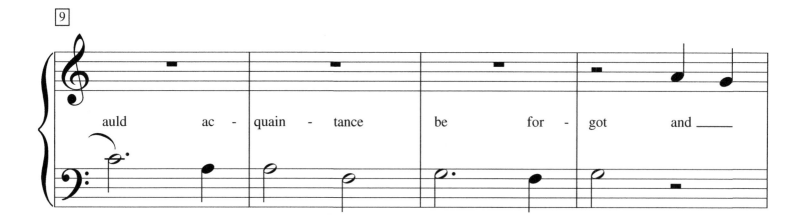

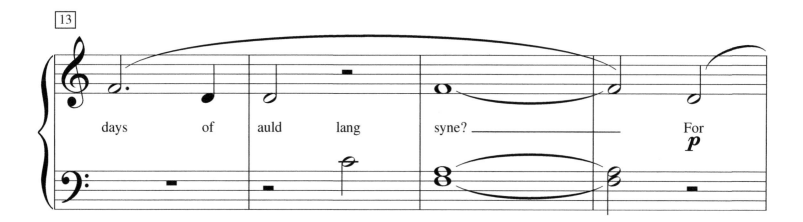

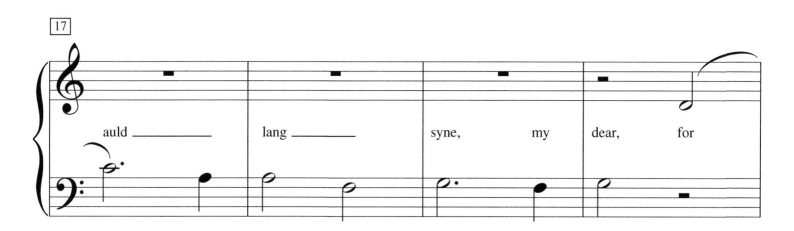

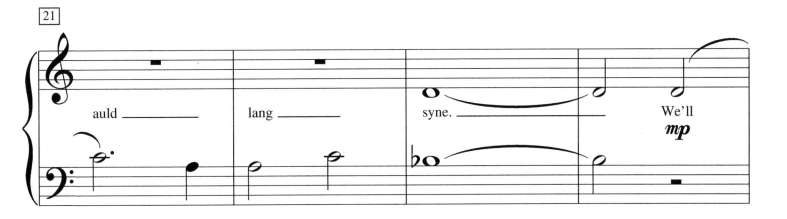

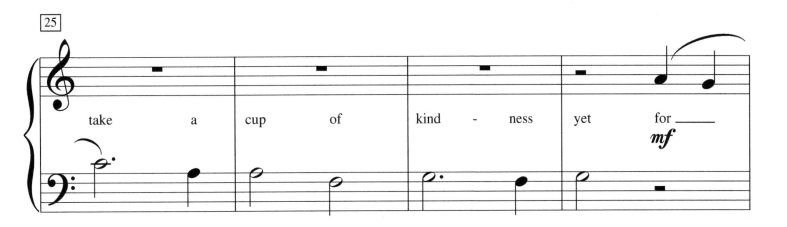

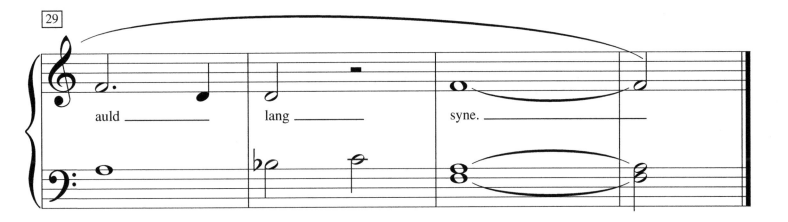

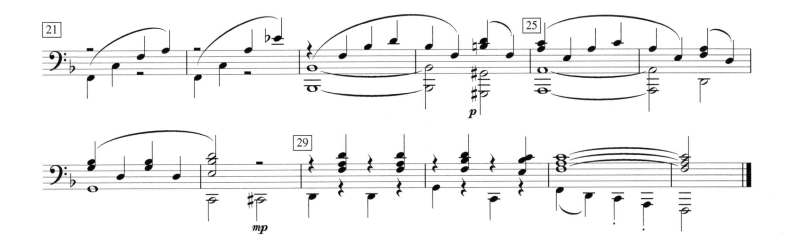

He Is Born, the Holy Child

Traditional French Carol
Arranged by Mona Rejino

Brightly (♩ = 120)

He is born, the ___ ho - ly Child, play the ___ o - boe and

bag - pipes mer - ri - ly. He is born, the ___ ho - ly Child, sing we all of the

Accompaniment (Student plays one octave higher than written.) **TRACKS 15/16**

Brightly (♩ = 120)

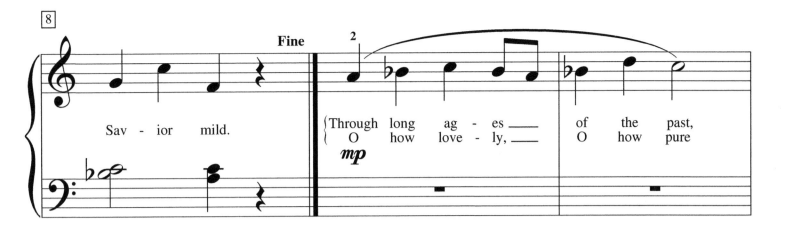

Sav - ior mild.

Through long ag - es _____ of the past,
O how love - ly, _____ O how pure

mp

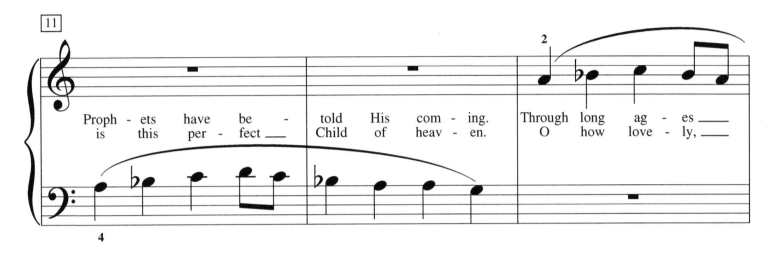

Proph - ets have be - told His com - ing.
is this per - fect _____ Child of heav - en.

Through long ag - es _____
O how love - ly, _____

of the past;
O how pure,

Now the time has _____ come at last!
Gra - cious gift of _____

1.

2.

D.C. al Fine

God to man!

Fine
p

D.C. al Fine

The Twelve Days of Christmas

Traditional English Carol
Arranged by Mona Rejino

Lively; in "two" (♩ = 96) TRACKS 17/18

On the first day of Christ-mas, my true love sent to

mf

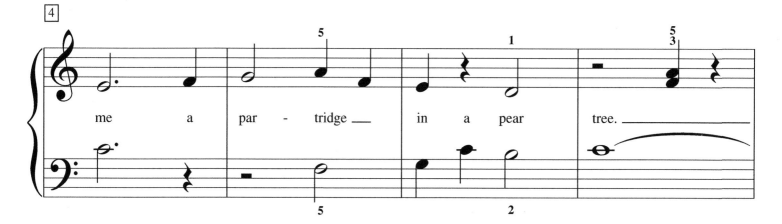

me a par-tridge ___ in a pear tree. ___

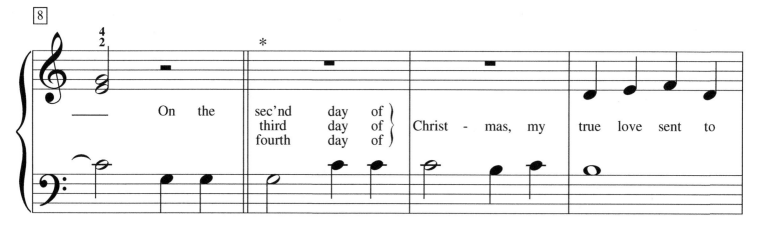

___ On the sec'nd day of
third day of
fourth day of } Christ-mas, my true love sent to

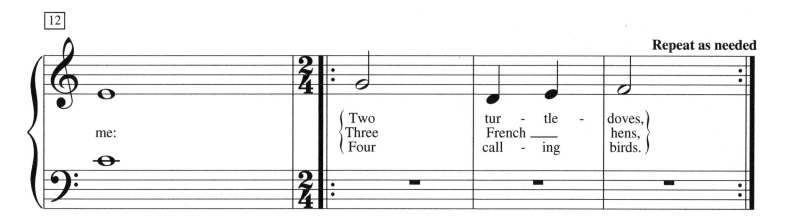

Repeat as needed

me: Two tur - tle - doves,
Three French ___ hens,
Four call - ing birds.

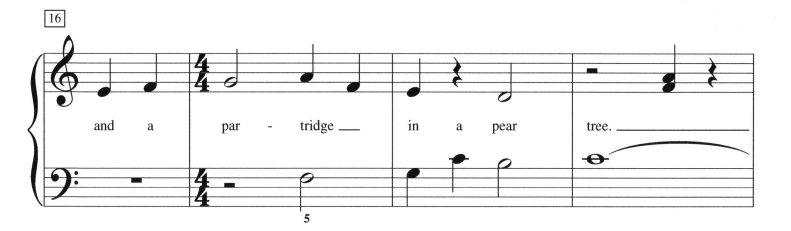

and a par - tridge ___ in a pear tree. ___

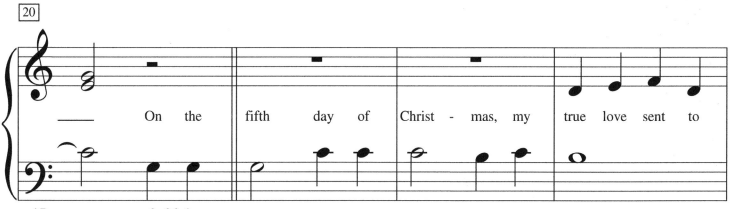

___ On the fifth day of Christ - mas, my true love sent to

*Repeat measures 9–20 for
the 3rd and 4th days.*

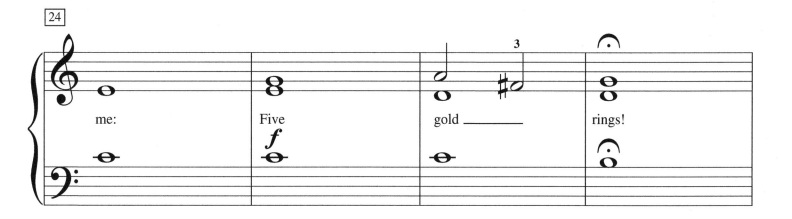

me: Five gold ___ rings!

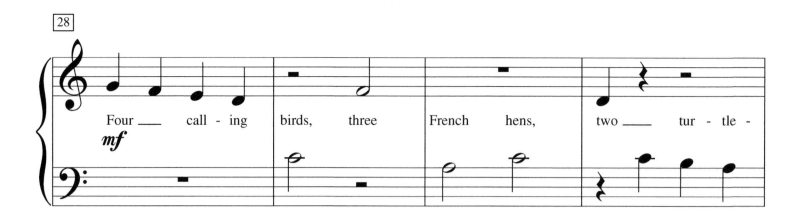

Four ___ call - ing birds, three French hens, two ___ tur - tle -

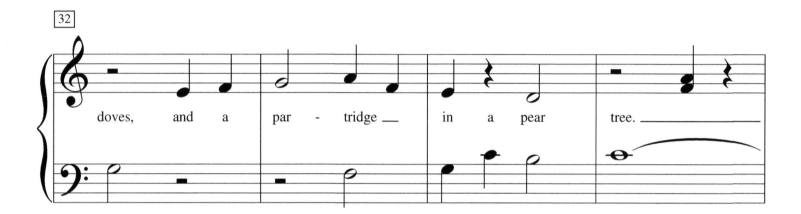

doves, and a par - tridge ___ in a pear tree. ___

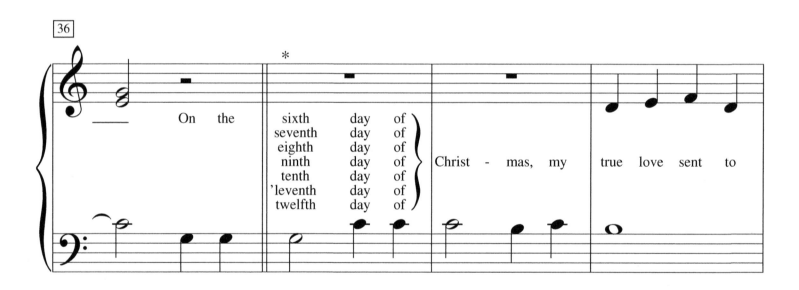

*

On the
sixth day of
seventh day of
eighth day of
ninth day of
tenth day of
'leventh day of
twelfth day of

Christ - mas, my true love sent to

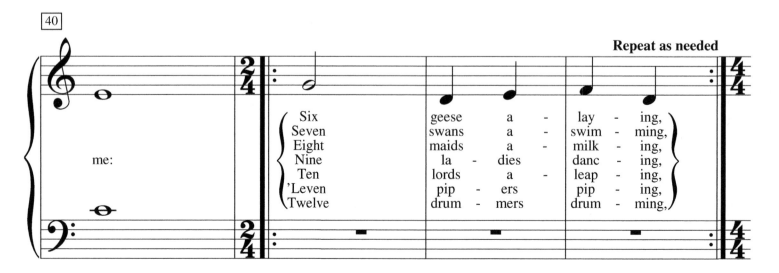

Repeat as needed

me:

Six geese a - lay - ing,
Seven swans a - swim - ming,
Eight maids a - milk - ing,
Nine la - dies danc - ing,
Ten lords a - leap - ing,
'Leven pip - ers pip - ing,
Twelve drum - mers drum - ming,

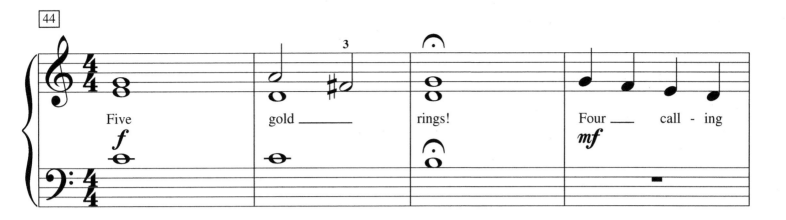

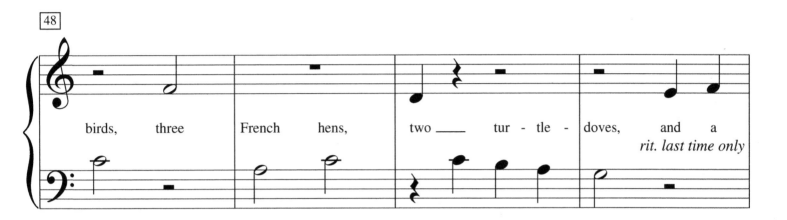

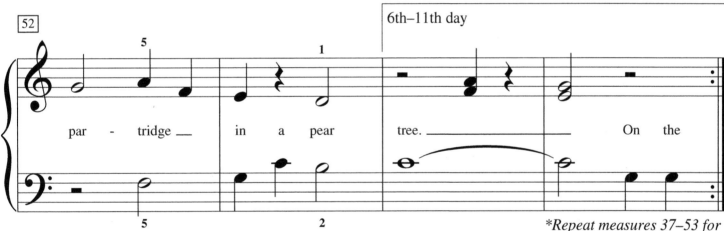

*Repeat measures 37–53 for
the 7th through 12th days.*

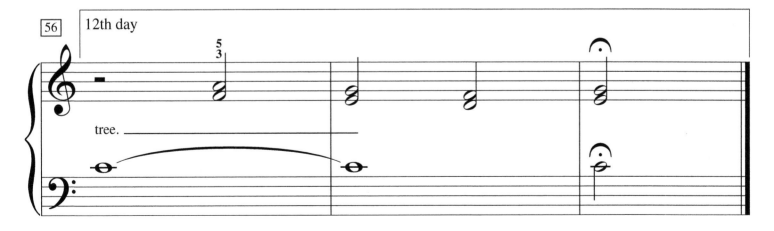

Hallelujah Chorus
from MESSIAH

By George Frideric Handel
Arranged by Fred Kern

Hal - le - lu - jah, Hal - le - lu - jah, Hal - le -

lu - jah, Hal - le - lu - jah, Hal - le - lu - jah,

Accompaniment (Student plays one octave higher than written.)

TRACKS 19/20

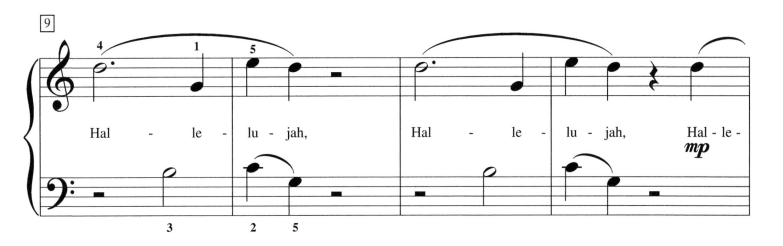

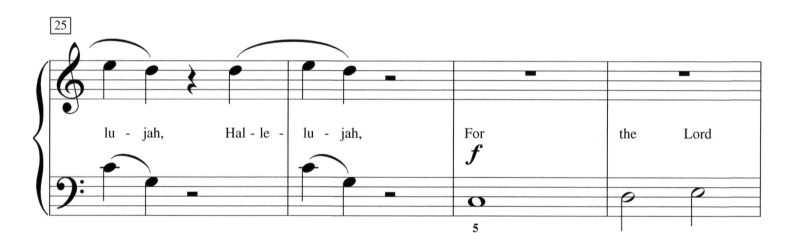

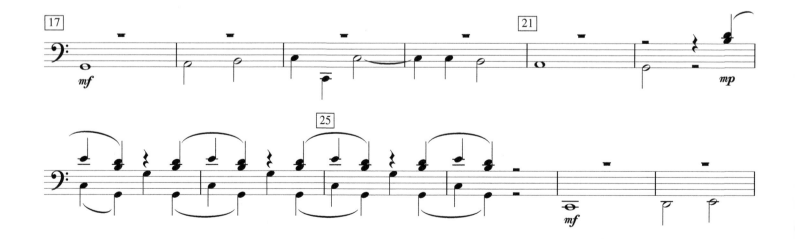

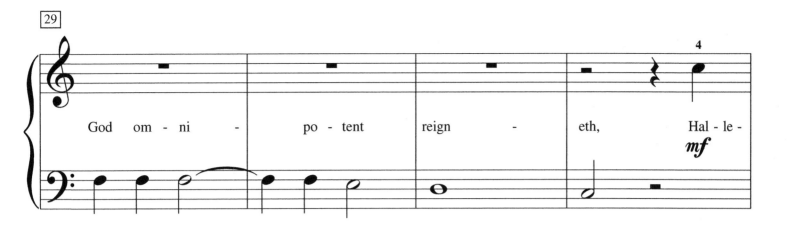

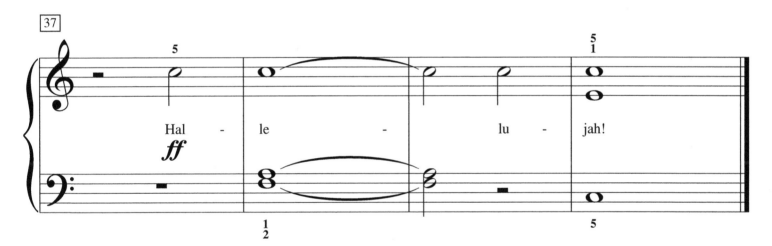

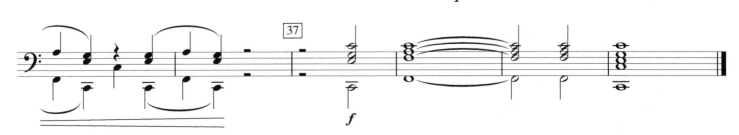